# **INTERVIEWING**

# INTERVIEWING

**LIZ EDWARDS**

**THE INDUSTRIAL SOCIETY**

First published 1997 by
The Industrial Society
48 Bryanston Square
London W1H 7LN
Tel. 0171 262 2401

© The Industrial Society 1997

ISBN 1 85835 5001

All rights reserved. No part of this publication may be reproduced, stored in a retrieval system or transmitted, in any form or by any means, electronic, mechanical, photocopying, recording and/or otherwise without the prior written permission of the publishers. This book may not be lent, resold, hired out or otherwise disposed of by way of trade in any form, binding or cover other than that in which it is published without prior consent of the publishers.

Typeset by: GCS
Printed by: Page Brothers Ltd
Cover Design: Rhodes Design

The Industrial Society is a Registered Charity No. 290003

# contents

**Foreword** ix

**Introduction** xi
  What is an interview? xi
  Why not play it by ear? xii

**1 Generic interview issues** 1
  Objectives 1

  Planning and preparation 3
    Why am I doing it? 4
    Who is the interviewee? 4
    Where will I do it? 4
    How will I do it? 5
    What will I need? 5

  Interviewing skills 5
    Questioning 6
    Active listening 9
    Talking 11
    Building a rapport 12

  General interviewing checklist 12

## 2 The selection interview — 14
Cost — 14

Objective — 15

Planning and preparation — 16

Conducting the interview — 19

Skills — 19
- Questioning — 19
- Active listening — 21
- Talking — 21
- Building a rapport — 22
- Making notes — 23
- Notetaking tips — 24
- Looking around — 25

Decision making — 26

References — 27

Selection interviewing checklist — 28

## 3 The counselling interview — 30
Objective — 30

Preparation — 30

Skills — 31
- Active listening — 32
- Questioning — 33
- Talking — 34
- Building a rapport — 34

Responsibilities — 35

Follow up — 36

Counselling interview checklist — 36

## CONTENTS

**4 The grievance interview** — 38
Objective — 38

Preparation — 39

Skills — 40
    Active listening — 40
    Questioning — 41
    Talking — 41
    Making notes — 42
    Emotion — 42

Outcome — 42

Follow up — 43

Grievance interview checklist — 43

**5 The disciplinary interview** — 45
Objective — 46

Preparation — 46

Skills — 47
    Active listening — 47
    Questioning — 48
    Talking — 48

Making a decision — 49

Follow up — 49

Disciplinary interview checklist — 50

**6 The appraisal interview** — 52
Objective — 53

Preparation — 54

| | |
|---|---|
| Skills | 56 |
|     Questioning | 56 |
|     Active listening | 56 |
|     Talking | 57 |
|     Action planning | 57 |
|     Building a rapport | 57 |
| Follow up | 58 |
| Appraisal interview checklist | 59 |
| **7 The exit interview** | **61** |
| Objective | 62 |
| Preparation | 62 |
| Skills | 62 |
|     Questioning | 62 |
|     Active listening | 63 |
|     Talking | 63 |
| Follow up | 63 |
| The exit interview checklist | 64 |
| **Appendix 1: Job description framework** | **65** |
| **Appendix 2: Person specification framework** | **66** |
| **Appendix 3: Interview assessment form framework** | **70** |
| **Appendix 4: Key items for inclusion in an application form** | **72** |
| **Appendix 5: Legislation affecting the interview process** | **73** |

# foreword

This book is for all of us who are in the business of talking to people with a purpose: all who manage, supervise, recruit, select. Our purposes will differ — to find the right person for the job, to help an individual to improve performance, to understand the reasons for a grievance — but the essential skills remain the same.

The Industrial Society has spent many years developing its work in communication skills and has helped a considerable number of people to become more effective and professional interviewers. It is both sensible and good business sense for organisations to have informed, capable individuals who can carry out the interview process fairly and correctly. This book offers practical, straightforward advice to all of us who need to develop our interviewing skills.

YVONNE BENNION
Policy Director

# introduction

The objective of this book is to set out some clear, practical guidelines for anyone about to conduct an interview. The general section looks at skills needed for all types of interviews; individual sections look in more depth at different types of interview:

- selection
- counselling
- grievance
- disciplinary
- appraisal
- exit.

You can use the book for a general browse through interviewing or alternatively for a specific application.

## What is an interview?

There are many ways to describe an interview — depending on the situation. However, for the purpose of this guide, we suggest it is:

'A discussion between people, with an objective, where one party is responsible for achieving that objective'.

In other words, an interview is a conversation with a purpose. The key point, however, is that the interviewer is responsible for managing the conversation and achieving the required outcome.

## Why not play it by ear?

The interview is a key part of a manager's role — whatever type of interview it may be. Getting it wrong could have serious implications: for the individual, the manager and the organisation.

There is no substitute for knowledge and experience combined with a professional attitude. Good interviewers will make sure they have a foundation of knowledge which they can apply in practice. This enables them to learn from their own experience, but, at the same time, they will listen to advice and pick up suggestions and advice where ever they can. This book aims to give you some well-used and effective tips to ensure that you:

- combine knowledge and professionalism
- avoid expensive mistakes through inadequate interviewing
- do not discriminate during an interview.

So, playing by ear may be okay where making mistakes or bad habits don't matter too much (such as learning to play the piano for fun; taking up golf as a hobby. It is not okay where people are involved: people are an organisation's main asset and should be treated as such.

# generic interview issues

This section looks at those generic areas that apply to all interviews.

## Objectives

Objectives are essential for an interviewer. Like a motorist without a destination: if you don't know where you want to go, how will you know when you get there? You cannot control and plan an interview if you don't know what you are aiming at: nor will you know if you have achieved your objective, if you are uncertain what it was in the first place. Like a motorist, you may have:

- the transport to get you there (the interview)
- the map to guide you (a plan)

but without a clear idea of the destination (objective) you are unlikely to succeed.

You may be lucky, of course: like the motorist who arrives by accident at the right destination, you achieve the unrecognised objective occasionally. But ... more often than not, you and the motorist are likely to go round and round aimlessly!

It is important to clarify what your objective is as this will determine your whole approach and the type of interview to use.

| *Type of interview* | *Objective* |
| --- | --- |
| Selection | To select the best available person for the job |
| Counselling | To listen to an individual's problem which may affect his/her work. To help that individual to find a solution to that problem, act on it or come to terms with the problem |
| Grievance | To enable an individual to air complaints; discover the causes of dissatisfaction and, where possible, remove them |
| Disciplinary | To discuss with an individual mistakes or inappropriate behaviour which need correcting and identifying ways in which specific improvements can be made |
| Appraisal | Usually a two-way discussion on a person's performance over a given period to:<br>• check achievement of competencies/outcomes<br>• assess performance including strengths, weaknesses and needs |

GENERIC INTERVIEW ISSUES

|  |  |
|---|---|
|  | • identify areas for development and improvement; ways of overcoming weaknesses |
| Exit | To get feedback on an individual's reason for resigning. This will assist in order to:<br>• improve the recruitment/ selection and development process<br>• deal with any weaknesses in the organisational system<br>• improve the organisation image with the employee<br>• change the individual's mind, if appropriate. |

## Planning and preparation

*'If you fail to plan, you plan to fail'*

Interviews should be planned: not just because an interviewer should be prepared, but more importantly, because:

- there is a need to be fair and equitable and work within the law
- interviews are more likely to succeed if carried out with some effort in advance.

Obviously, there are some situations where it is difficult to do any planning. For example: if someone drops in unexpectedly for a chat about a problem.

3

If you have an interview to carry out, ask yourself some questions:

### WHY AM I DOING IT?
Identify the objective of the interview and the approach you should adopt. This should clarify how long the interview should last.

### WHO IS THE INTERVIEWEE?
Identify the knowledge you have about the interviewee. Then identify any further information or special requirements you need in relation to that person.

For example: personal files, references, loop system or interpreter should the individual have either a hearing difficulty or be profoundly deaf.

### WHERE WILL I DO IT?
Identify a suitable room (if there is a choice). It should be big enough and adequate for your purposes. For example: there needs to be adequate access if the interviewee has a physical disability; it should be pleasant and not too stark.

Think about the layout. For example: if a desk is used, will you sit either side or side by side; will you use a coffee table?

Watch out for potential distractions. For example: creaking desks, doors and external traffic noises (these are picked up by a loop system and make it extremely difficult for hearing impaired individuals); direct sunlight in an individual's eyes may be intimidating. Make sure there won't be any interruptions, by either people or telephones.

GENERIC INTERVIEW ISSUES

### HOW WILL I DO IT?

Identify the approach you should adopt once you have taken into account the objective, the knowledge and any special requirements of the interviewee.

### WHAT WILL I NEED?

Identify the resources you need.

For example: an interpreter (for someone who is profoundly deaf or whose English is poor); a loop system (for a hearing impaired individual); translation of documents into Braille (for a sight impaired person) or another language.

What materials will you need (company rules, personal files, application forms, job descriptions, person specifications)?

Identify any further information needed (the limits of your authority; any background data or statistics).

## Interviewing skills

A good interviewer needs to be able to control the progress of the discussion to:

- facilitate a common understanding
- enable two-way communication
- achieve the objective of the interview.

The main skills needed for this process are communication skills.

## QUESTIONING

Have you ever gone round and round in circles, despite asking lots of questions? Questioning is useful only if you ask the right questions.

Think first and identify the most effective way to phrase a question before you ask it.

Some types of questions can be useful:

| Type of question | Explanation and example | Usage |
| --- | --- | --- |
| Open | Questions that usually cannot be answered by 'yes' or 'no'. *'Tell me about the time you spent ...'* | They encourage the interviewee to expand and do more talking. They may also elicit feelings and attitudes as well as facts. Open questions begin with 'Tell me..?, Who?, When?, What?, Where?, How?, Why?'. Be careful with questions beginning with 'Why?': in some situations they may seem aggressive. |
| Closed | Questions that usually require only a 'yes' or 'no'. *'I understand from what you've been saying that you would like to change departments. Is that correct?'* | It can be used to summarise, bringing the conversation back on track, if it has wandered. It enables the interviewer to tie up one part and move onto the next. It also helps to check mutual understanding. |

# GENERIC INTERVIEW ISSUES

| Type of question | Explanation and example | Usage |
|---|---|---|
| Reflective | Reflects a statement/question by rephrasing it and sending it back to the interviewee. Interviewee: *'I have had a difficult time in that department'*. Interviewer: *'So, you feel that things haven't been easy for you in Marketing?'* | It gives the interviewee the opportunity to think about what he/she has just said. It also helps to keep him/her talking and often gets more information on a subject. It also avoids personal involvement if the interviewer is asked a direct question and answering it might not be wise. It is particularly useful in a counselling interview. |
| Probing | Investigates further. *'When you took that action, what was the outcome?'* | Used to steer the conversation down a narrow path in order to get more in depth information. |
| Checking | It checks understanding. *'Is that acceptable?'* | Avoids misunderstanding and possible future disagreement. |
| Hypothetical | To make a supposition about the future. *'How would you deal with....?'* | Used to test reactions and speed of thinking in dealing with problems. However, in a selection interview, an experienced person may have a 'pat' answer ready. |

# INTERVIEWING

| Type of question | Explanation and example | Usage |
|---|---|---|
| Behavioural | Used to find out how situations were handled. *'When you led the project, how did you tackle the problem of. ...?'* | Useful in selection interviewing to establish how an interviewee behaved in previous roles and favoured by some interviewers over hypothetical questioning. |
| Specific | Used to get specific information. *'When did you change jobs?'* | This type of question is useful for checking facts and getting decisions. There is only one correct answer to a specific question. Can be used with a talkative interviewee or a 'waffler'. The only way of getting the facts you need may be to ask specific questions. |

There are also one or two question types that you should be careful about:

| Type of question | Explanation and example | Likely effect/usage |
|---|---|---|
| Leading | It signals the response you want. *'So you are good at dealing with people?'* | The interviewee may agree through nervousness, confusion, a lack of attention, etc. However, it can be used sparingly on occasions. For example: a test question to check a person's knowledge and |

# GENERIC INTERVIEW ISSUES

| Type of question | Explanation and example | Likely effect/usage |
|---|---|---|
| | | attitudes; an easy question in the initial stages of an interview to settle a person in. |
| Multiple | A series of questions all in one sentence. 'Where did you take ... and tell me why ...what do you think?' | The interviewee is baffled and may not know which question to answer first. An experienced interviewee will answer the question that suits him/her best. |

A good interviewer will alternate the questions to develop the appropriate style of interview. In most interviews, the interviewer needs to obtain both facts and feelings/attitudes, so a combination of questions is normally needed.

## ACTIVE LISTENING

Most people don't listen properly: often they are thinking about what they want to say next rather than assimilating what is being said. Listening effectively is as important as asking the right questions. It is only by listening that an interviewer can work out what the next question should be. An interviewer needs to listen and observe very closely to pick up clues if he/she hasn't received enough information or suspects there is something odd about the answer. However, an interview is a two-way process: the interviewee needs to be encouraged to talk.

All of this calls for active listening. This is a combination of:

- listening
- using verbal and non verbal skills
- observing.

*Listen* to and analyse what is being said. *Listen* for what is *not* said. Pick up general points for more detailed expansion and identify discrepancies. *Listen* to how things are being said (tone of voice). *Watch* for emphasis or contradiction by observing the interviewee's body language (facial expressions; gestures; posture and eye-contact). If the interviewee has a disability, this may not be appropriate. Also, a lot of eye contact is not appropriate in some cultures (Japanese people look at others very little). Body language can also be used to gauge the person's feeling (this may not be appropriate if the interviewee has a physical disability).

In addition to the importance of the listening itself, it is also essential *to be seen to be listening*. This helps to establish and maintain rapport as well as encouraging the interviewee. Use non-verbal gestures to encourage: eye contact, open posture, facial and hand gestures (with a sight impaired person some of these won't apply).

Eye contact is the major way to show you are listening: unless you use it, the other person may feel cut off. However, too much eye contact can feel threatening and cause a loss of confidence. If the other person appears to be reacting uncomfortably, look away. Most of us get the balance right in normal conversation naturally. The trouble with

## GENERIC INTERVIEW ISSUES

interviews is that most of us tend to get nervous and react nervously — this may be more pronounced when dealing with an interviewee who has a physical disability (involuntary twitching or a facial disfigurement can be disconcerting).

Let the interviewee know you are listening by acknowledging: 'yes','I see', 'I understand', 'mm', 'ah'. (particularly important with a sight impaired interviewee).

### TALKING

The majority of the talking should come from the interviewee. The amount will differ depending on the type of interview.

As an interviewer, you should not talk for the sake of it: the more you do, the less the other person can.

You may need to supply information to direct the interview. This could be to:

- *clarify misunderstandings* that may have arisen
- *give information* to enable the interviewee to understand the situation
- *give reassurance* in certain circumstances.

A good interviewer uses interim and final summaries:

- *interim:* to keep control and to bring the conversation 'back on track'; as a signpost showing where it has been and where it is going next
- *final:* to give a positive finish and make clear the final and future action to both parties.

## BUILDING A RAPPORT

Using *communication skills* effectively enables an interviewer to carry out the process more successfully and help to build a rapport with the interviewee.

Other ways to help break down barriers are:

- through *preparation* (it can be extremely off-putting if an interviewer spends the first part of an interview reading background information)
- by *controlling* the interview throughout (this can give the interviewee the confidence that something is to be achieved as a result of the interview)
- by making sure the *purpose, outcome* and *length* of the interview are stated quite clearly (this clarifies for the interviewee what is to be achieved and how long it will take and enables him/her to relax)
- through showing interest (common understanding and relaxation can be difficult to achieve but are essential to avoid the failure of the interview). This also enables the development of empathy — an understanding of the other person's feelings in a situation.

# General interviewing checklist

### OBJECTIVE
What do I want to achieve by the end of this interview?

## GENERIC INTERVIEW ISSUES

### PLANNING AND PREPARATION

Have I got the answers to the following questions:

- Who is the interviewee?
- How will I do the interview?
- Where will I do the interview?
- What will I need?

### SKILLS

How will I use my skills of:

- questioning?
- active listening?
- talking?
- summarising
- building rapport?

Will I be able to control the interview and achieve the aims of:

- enabling a common understanding?
- ensuring two way communication?
- achieving the objective?

### FOLLOW UP

Have I taken any action that was agreed? If not, by when do I need to take the action?

# 2 the selection interview

Selection interviewing remains the most popular method for recruiting new staff although more and more organisations are combining it with other selection methods (application forms; ability/ aptitude tests; assessment centres). Carrying out a selection interview is one of the most important jobs a manager can do, and should be treated as such. The success of an organisation depends upon the work of the individuals within it — every misplaced person detracts from its success. The purpose of selection interviews is to get the right people to take the organisation forward. The responsibility is yours and yours alone to make the best selection; give it the respect it deserves.

## Cost

The cost of recruitment and selection can be high. The cost of incorrect selection is likely to be much higher. There are a number of obvious expenses:

- the initial recruitment process
- the interviewer's time

- training and development
- starting the cycle again: more recruitment, more interviewer time, more training and development.

The wrong person in a job can cause less obvious costs to mount up. If someone is not productive, this can cause errors, missed deadlines, reduced standards and poor customer service. All of these have both quality and cost implications.

Team difficulties can also be an indirect expense. If someone is not pulling his/her weight in a team it adds pressure to the others. This can lead to resentment and demotivation, resulting in low morale and an overall reduction in standards. Even if an individual is perfectly capable of doing the job, his/her personality may clash with some or all of the team. This also causes demotivation and may even result in others resigning in extreme circumstances. But beware of always recruiting the same type of person, or allowing fears about a team's reactions to cause you to discriminate unlawfully.

## Objective

A selection interview is a two-way discussion.

The main objective is two-fold: firstly, to identify those candidates who would be able and willing to do the job and secondly, to select the best person for that job.

Two other objectives are:

- to give a good impression of the organisation to all the applicants

- to give the candidates the opportunity to find out about the organisation, the job and the conditions.

A selection interview is, to some extent, a public relations exercise. The candidates leave with an impression of the organisation. That impression is derived, in the main, from the interviewers. You, as an interviewer, are the organisation as far as the candidate is concerned. Give a bad impression and it doesn't take too long to get around. It should be remembered that negative impressions far outweigh positive ones and last longer!

## Planning and preparation

Much of the success of a selection interview depends on good planning and preparation. The first step is to establish what the job involves and what sort of person could fulfil it. Therefore, a job description and a person specification need to be prepared.

- A *job description* should identify the purpose, scope, responsibilities and key competencies/ tasks/outcomes of the job. It is a practical document which should be updated as a job changes. (See Appendix 1 for an example framework.)
- A *person specification* gives a word picture of the ideal person for the job based on a plan — usually a seven or five point list. (See Appendix 2 for an example seven-point plan.) It can be useful also

in pinpointing specific attributes particularly when others methods of assessment are being used also such as questionnaires and tests. When drawing up a person specification, you must take care to ensure that the specification's criteria don't discriminate (directly or indirectly) against women, men, ethnic minorities, disabled people, etc.

The interview structure needs planning and any information about the candidate read in advance. Time should be taken to compare the candidate information (CV/application form) with the job description and the person specification outlines. (See Appendix 4: what to include in an application form.) This should enable an interview plan to be sketched out: a list of areas which might need further exploration or clarification. However, an interview plan shouldn't be a rigid timetable.

Questioning should be planned to assess competence, knowledge and attitudes. The 'ideal person' profiled in the person specification will help to clarify the form that questions should take. It is worth drawing up an assessment system which can be based on the person specification. This will enable the comparison of candidates against the ideal rather than each other and the making of informed decisions based on identified factors rather than 'gut' feelings. (See Appendix 3 for an example framework.)

If more than one interviewer is involved, then the planning will need to include identification of which areas will be covered by whom and who will be responsible for introductions and conclusions.

If you are going to conduct selection interviews, you will need to think about the environment.

- Will the candidate be greeted at reception?
- Is the room layout suitable?
- Have refreshments been arranged?
- Will interruptions/delays be avoided?
- Will candidates have adequate access (for wheelchairs, dogs)?
- Will you need communication or language support (interpreter, loop system, translator)?

If you are doing more than one interview, you will need to ensure that you have structured the time adequately.

- Have you allocated time to read through the applications beforehand?
- Has enough time been allowed between interviews to write up notes and/or review?

Have you gathered together any other relevant information (organisational structure; products/services; details of other sites/locations or associated companies; benefits and conditions, etc.)?

You must also be up to date with current legislation to ensure that equality of opportunity is given and that you are fair and unbiased with every candidate.

(See Appendix 5 for a list of the relevant areas which apply.)

THE SELECTION INTERVIEW

## Conducting the interview

An interview is like a presentation: it works best if it has a beginning, a middle and an end. The *beginning* is for scene setting: putting the candidate at ease by making introductions, explaining the structure and length of the interview as well as identifying the purpose. The aim of the *middle* section is to find out if the candidate can do the job and will fit into the team. This is where structured, but not rigid, questioning should be used based on the person specification. The *end* should be used to summarise discussions, enable candidates to ask any questions or seek further clarification as well as explain the next steps.

## Skills

The candidates should be doing the majority of the talking: approximately 70%. A good interviewer will use his/her communication skills to achieve this.

QUESTIONING
Some types of questions are more useful than others. You should be:

- asking *open* questions to get the conversation going and encourage the candidate to talk
- using *specific* or *closed* questions to make sure that all the facts are drawn out

- asking *behavioural* questions to clarify how the individual solved problems, dealt with difficulties or applied principles
- having *hypothetical* questions ready prepared to test how the individual would think through and approach a problem as well using them to test knowledge
- using *probing* questions to obtain further details. Never accept a partial answer or one that dodges a question. If you are suspicious of an answer, probe by either phrasing it differently and asking a further question to find out more.

Both hypothetical and behavioural questions are more appropriate in the 'middle' of the interview. If they are asked at the beginning when candidates haven't had the opportunity to settle in, they may clam up through nervousness and be unable to continue effectively. Whilst it is important to ask the *right* questions, it is equally important *not* to ask discriminatory questions. Information gathering should be related to the job you wish to fill and the candidate's ability to do that job.

- You *cannot ask* a person from an ethnic minority whether his/her English is 'up to the job'. You *may ask* all candidates for proof of their ability in written English (GCSE/'A' level/ Degree or an equivalent standard gained in another country) providing it is needed for the job.
- You *cannot ask* some candidates about their arrangements for taking care of children. However, you *may ask* all candidates *'Do the hours of work pose any problems for you?'*

- You *cannot ask* a disabled candidate if he/she can cope with the job. You *may ask* all candidates 'Would you be physically able to do the job?'

## ACTIVE LISTENING

It is only through careful listening, giving encouragement and using appropriate body language that an interviewer can get the maximum from the candidate. If you are interviewing candidates:

- *listen* carefully to pick up inconsistencies and assimilate information from what is being said and how it is being said
- *observe body language*, where appropriate, to check that it is in congruence with what is being said
- *use your own body language* to encourage the candidate
- *use* silence to give the person time to think.

## TALKING

This is a combination of summarising and giving information. If you are carrying out a selection interview:

- *summarise* to keep the discussion on track. *Interim* summaries are useful when one subject area has been concluded. A *final* summary leaves the candidate with a good impression of the organisation: whether or not he/she is offered the job. Confirm the areas that have been covered during the interview and give the candidates the opportunity to ask any questions of their own. You may wish also to clarify if the candidate is interested still in the post

- *give appropriate information.* The interview is a two-way process. Whilst you want to know if the candidate can do the job, likewise he/she wants to know if the job is right for him/her. This section will come towards the end of the interview. You should ensure that the candidate has a full, honest description of the job.

If the location is a room with 20 other people and no windows — say so. It is better to lose the individual at this stage than to appoint someone and he/she leaves within a few months of starting. However, there is little to be gained by exaggerating the problem — if you make that room sound a dank dungeon — nobody will want to work there! (It may be appropriate to give candidates the opportunity to look round the organisation, work area and meet potential colleagues. See 'Looking around').

Other areas of information that might be covered are: the organisation and its ethos; salary; benefits and other terms and conditions.

You should explain what happens next: whether there are further interviews; when candidates are likely to hear from the organisation; giving feedback on tests or job shadowing, if appropriate. Thank the candidate for his/her time before shaking hands and showing him/her out.

## BUILDING A RAPPORT

This is crucial in the selection interview. If a candidate is helped to relax quickly, the interviewer is more likely to get a worthwhile response. The length of time it takes and how difficult it is will depend on:

# THE SELECTION INTERVIEW

- the age, experience and confidence of the candidate
- the skill of the interviewer in making a positive impression and facilitating the process.

Some tips to assist you when you are interviewing:

- show the candidate that you are in control and well organised
- make sure the layout and facilities in the room are both suitable and conducive to the process (a large table between you and the candidates reduces rapport; seating should be accessible and at the same level; strong sunlight/glaring lights shouldn't be in the candidates' eyes; heating should be comfortable; access must be suitable for disabled candidates)
- offer refreshments (make sure there is somewhere to put the cup/glass)
- avoid:
  — first impressions (judging quickly and ignoring contradictory information)
  — the 'halo' effect (being over-impressed by certain qualities; same leisure pursuits, nationality)
  — the 'contrast' effect (rating an average candidate lower who comes after an outstanding person).

## MAKING NOTES

*'A short pencil is more effective than a long memory'*

Most people find listening difficult and remembering what they have heard even more of a challenge!

Making notes enables an interviewer to go back to interesting points or inconsistencies that need probing later. If they don't jot things down, the likelihood is they won't recall them until after the candidate has left.

Notes are useful (and often necessary) to help in the final assessment of the candidates. How can interviewers assess if they cannot remember what was said and how they felt about it?

A note should also be made of the reasons for appointing, or not appointing, a candidate. This may be important should there be a challenge for direct or indirect discrimination (on the grounds of race, sex, disability, etc. See Appendix 5).

If a candidate is not a British National, it is necessary, at this stage, to ask for a 'documented National Insurance number' or other documents establishing his/her legal entitlement to work in the United Kingdom. A note will have to be made, particularly if a follow up is necessary to ensure the document is forthcoming. This is expected under the Asylum and Immigration Act 1996. (See Appendix 5.)

Notes should be kept for a minimum of six months in the case of unsuccessful external candidates and preferably longer for successful candidates or unsuccessful internal candidates.

### NOTETAKING TIPS

Notetaking can be distracting for candidates so:

- always ask them at the outset if they mind you taking notes
- don't try to put everything down — just key words or facts

# THE SELECTION INTERVIEW

- try to sit so that they cannot see what you are writing
- make a point of writing down notes when they are highlighting information they think is important
- maintain eye contact with them — don't allow the notes to become more important than them
- beware of doodling or writing anything contentious that could be challenged later!

## LOOKING AROUND

You may wish to give candidates a tour of the building where they will work, including the specific area in which they would be located. It has three advantages:

- if the candidate wouldn't be happy, or prepared, to work in the environment, you can find that out quickly. For example: a large company in West London interviewed a secretary for a job. The interview took place in a room on the ground floor. When she arrived for her first day at work, she discovered she would be working on the twelfth floor. She suffered from claustrophobia and could not use the lift; she left the same day
- it could be useful to introduce the candidates to the other people in the team/department/section to see how they react to those people they would be working with. Be warned: firstly, if this is to be taken into account in the selection process, then the candidate should be told. Secondly, any comments from those people with whom they might be working, are hearsay and should be treated as such. They should not be taken into account in the final decision

- it can be used to ascertain if a disabled person has adequate access or if adjustments or alterations would need to be carried out prior to his/her commencing work.

## Decision making

Following the interviews, make an assessment of the candidates. It is advisable to use some sort of system:

- complete a written report or a pre-printed assessment form. (See Appendix 3.)
- compare the candidates' assessments against the job description and person specification.

Avoid comparing the candidates against each other: that is not the purpose of the assessment.

Once you have made your selection, (a first and second choice and possibly another one for contingency) make a note on the remaining candidates' details as to why they hadn't been successful. Again, this sort of information is very useful should there be any queries or comeback.

Make a conditional offer (this may be dependent on references, medicals, examination results) to the first choice within the time limit set, if possible. Keep your second and third choice pending until a reply has been received to the offer. Do inform the other unsuccessful candidates as quickly as possible. It can be very distressing for candidates to wait; it is also unprofessional and does nothing for the image of the organisation. An offer letter should include:

- the title and/or the job description
- conditions of the offer (acceptable references; confirmation of qualification certificates; passing a medical examination)
- terms and conditions (salary, benefits, contractual obligations, pension — if applicable)
- action to be taken by the candidate (returning signed copy of letter; giving agreement to references being taken up; refraining from giving resignation to current employer until the conditions of the offer have been met)
- date of commencement
- hours of work, if applicable
- probationary period, if relevant.

Finally, make arrangements for the individual to start work (induction programme etc).

## References

Take up references, if possible, before making an offer of employment. This is essential for any candidate who will be working in a position of trust. Check references carefully, preferably by telephone, to ensure that they are genuine and accurate. Statements such as *'Susan works well under supervision'* should be considered carefully — often what is *not* said in a reference is more telling than what *is* said. Be specific — ensure that you get answers to the questions you are posing. Employers are more reluctant to give information than they used to be in case legal action is taken against them. However, as long as the information is factually correct, there shouldn't be a problem.

A reference from the current employer may be taken up after a conditional offer has been made.

## Selection interviewing checklist

OBJECTIVE
To select the best available person for the job.

PLANNING AND PREPARATION
- Review the legal implications of selection interviewing
- Make initial preparations (job description; person specification; an assessment) and accommodate any candidates' particular needs
- Plan questioning to assess competence, knowledge and attitudes
- Prepare interview plan
- Check that proposed questions will not be discriminatory
- Prepare an accessible room with suitable layout, taking account of any sensory or mobility impaired candidates
- Arrange refreshments and minimise interruptions/delays
- Schedule the interviews to allow time for each interview and between interviews
- Arrange technical or human support, if applicable
- Study the information (job description; person specification based on the job description; application form/curriculum vitae; test results, if applicable)
- Gather together all relevant data for the interview (job description; person specification; application

form/curriculum vitae; tests; application; interview assessment form; organisational information).

## SKILLS
- The communication skills needed are questioning; active listening; talking
- Other skills needed are building a rapport; notetaking.

## DECISION MAKING
- Update notes between interviews and complete assessments
- Make a decision based on the assessments and/or job description and person specification and select the best three candidates.

## FOLLOW UP
- Make a conditional offer to the first choice and include all the relevant points in the offer letter
- Inform the unsuccessful candidates
- Take up references
- Make the final arrangements for the new starter
- Inform the two other unsuccessful candidates once confirmation has been received from your first choice.

# 3 the counselling interview

Counselling is a necessary part of any manager's job. In the modern world, there seem to be more pressures on people. Many organisations are using professional counsellors for serious staff problems. However, quite frequently managers are the first 'port of call' for staff who need help and managers need to know how to deal with them. Problems may be related to people's work or their personal lives — both will affect the way they do their job.

## Objective

To assist an individual to:

- recognise and accept a problem
- reach a solution and take action.

## Preparation

Preparation isn't often possible. People sometimes 'pop in' to talk about a problem without warning. However, it is possible to be prepared in terms of

# THE COUNSELLING INTERVIEW

knowing what your role should, and shouldn't be. You are there to listen and help the person to solve the problem for themselves. <u>You are not there to give advice.</u>

When you do have some warning, there are some preparation steps you can take. You can:

- find an accessible room which is private and free from interruptions
- allow plenty of time before your next appointment
- read through the individual's file
- if you know what the problem is, check your own limits of authority in dealing with it
- gather together some specialist names and telephone numbers of people or organisations who might be useful to the person, particularly if the problem is beyond the person's expertise (Citizens Advice Bureaux; Social Services; Relate; Alcoholics Anonymous).

## Skills

In order to make a success of a counselling interview, you need to be able to get the confidence and trust of the interviewee before helping him/her to identify and explore the problem. Only then will you be able to assist him/her to find a solution. Remember: the purpose of the meeting is to identify the problem. It is not to offer solutions, give advice or make a judgement.

The main skills needed in a counselling interview are:

- active listening (initially to put the interviewee at ease and then to encourage the individual to talk through the problem)
- questioning (to help expand on and work through to the problem)
- talking (to summarise each stage)
- an ability to stay neutral and not take sides.

The first step will be to put the individual at ease — reassure him/her that what is being discussed will be treated in the strictest confidence and go no further.

## ACTIVE LISTENING

This is an occasion when talking by the interviewer takes even more of a 'back seat'.

Allow the interviewee to talk freely without interruptions. *Listen* to and analyse what is being said and how it is being said. *Listen* for what is *not* said. *Watch* the interviewee's body language (facial expressions; gestures; posture and eye-contact).

*Body language* can be very useful in this situation to help gauge the person's feeling. Remember, there are some exceptions (interviewees with disabilities, some ethnic minorities).

In addition to listening, it is also essential *to be seen to be listening*. Use non-verbal gestures to encourage: make eye contact, lean forward, use open palms, smile gently, keep an open posture. Also, make sure the interviewee knows you are listening by acknowledging: 'yes', 'I see', 'I understand', 'mm', 'ah'.

## QUESTIONING

The purpose of questioning should be:

- firstly, to help the interviewee to open up
- secondly, to enable him/her to reflect on what exactly the problem is
- thirdly, to think through alternatives which were not immediately apparent to him/her.

In this way, he/she should be able to come to some decision about the course of action to take.

If you are carrying out a counselling interview use:

- *open* questions initially to get the person talking about the problem. At a later stage, they may also be used to find out how the interviewee felt about things or situations. For example: 'What did you feel when....?' 'How did you feel after....?'
- *specific* questions to get to the core of the problem. Sometimes the real problem is not what the interviewer thought it was originally
- *reverse* questions to encourage people to examine their own thoughts and statements, avoiding your own commitment. For example:

| | |
|---|---|
| *interviewee:* | 'What do you think I can do?' |
| *interviewer:* | 'Well, what things do you think you could do?' |
| *interviewee:* | 'I don't know' |
| *interviewer:* | 'So, are you telling me you can't do anything?' |

*interviewee:*    'Well, I suppose I could either go on putting up with it, or leave home'

*interviewer:*    'You could but ... have you ever thought of talking it over with your partner or perhaps getting in touch with an organisation such as Relate before making that sort of decision?'

- *behavioural* questions to find out how the interviewee reacted. (This may indicate how she/he will behave in the future.)

## TALKING

The more talking the interviewer does, the less chance there is of sorting the problem. Ideally, the balance should be 90% interviewee and 10% interviewer.

However, this doesn't mean that you should clam up completely. You may have to give reassurance in certain circumstances. It will also be useful to summarise as you go along. Use:

- *interim summaries:* to clarify where you are and what has been covered before you move on
- *a final summary:* to give a positive finish and identify what the next stage will be. (This could be a further meeting; the interviewee getting some professional help or some other action.)

## BUILDING A RAPPORT

Try to understand the interviewee's position and let him/her know that you do. However, giving sympathy can be most unproductive. Most people require a solid post to lean on, not somebody to wallow in the problem with them. Too much sympathy concentrates on the emotions rather than on a logical solution that will help.

It may be necessary for the interviewee to release pent-up emotions before he/she is able to think logically. An interviewer needs to be able to deal with that emotion whilst remaining calm and neutral. It is important not to be judgmental and remain objective throughout.

Objectivity has to be coupled with being empathetic: an understanding of the interviewee's feelings in the situation (by making the interviewee aware that you both understand his/her feelings and are positive about sharing the issue).

Stress that the problem is important to you: many people are afraid of just being a nuisance and taking up valuable time. Don't continually check your watch or the clock (take your watch off and put it somewhere you can see it without being obtrusive).

# Responsibilities

The problem is not yours! Once it has been identified and clarified, you need to make sure that the interviewee knows and accepts that it is his/her responsibility. You will also want to help him/her to think about a suitable solution. For example: *'Now that you can see what the problem is, what do you want to do about it?'*

If he/she has a number of options to choose from, you may also need to help him/her to select the most appropriate one. Remember: you are there to assist not decide for the interviewee. Give the interviewee the menu rather than making the selection yourself. You shouldn't say *'You should go and see Social Services'*; you could say *'Social Services have helped people in a similar situation'*.

## Follow up

Always follow up a counselling interview. Even if the problem was solved completely during the interview, you should check up with the interviewee over the next few weeks to ascertain if everything is all right. If the problem hasn't resolved itself, you may need to arrange another meeting or alternatively, suggest the individual gets some professional help.

Checking up is important for three reasons:

- it assures interviewees that you do care and that you didn't just forget the whole thing once they had gone out the door

- it encourages people to take action if they know that someone cares enough to find out about what has happened

- it gives you feedback as to whether the problem has resolved itself or not and so enable you to manage or support that person more effectively.

## Counselling interview checklist

### OBJECTIVE
To enable someone to recognise and accept a problem, reach a solution and take action.

# THE COUNSELLING INTERVIEW

## PREPARATION
- Ensure privacy and adequate time
- Check limits of own authority
- Study individual's file
- Keep a record of specialists who could help
- Plan approach according to the individual.

## SKILLS
Use:
- active listening to put interviewee at ease and encourage the individual to talk
- questioning to help the person work through to the problem
- talking to summarise each stage.

Be empathetic throughout by demonstrating understanding and appreciation of how the individual feels.

## RESPONSIBILITIES
Ensure the interviewee accepts responsibility for the problem and any future action.

## FOLLOW UP
- Arrange further interview to check developments, if appropriate
- Check how the interviewee is progressing
- If the problem had effected the individual's work, assess whether or not the situation has improved.

# 4 the grievance interview

A grievance is any dissatisfaction that employees might have with the organisation or in their relationships with people within it. The objective is similar to that of a counselling interview, although the emphasis is quite different. In the counselling situation, help is given to enable the individual to come to his/her own conclusions. In a grievance interview, a complaint has been made and needs to be investigated either informally or through a formal grievance procedure. It is essential to ensure that the grievance is handled by the most appropriate person from the outset and that any grievance is taken seriously and handled sensitively, no matter how frivolous it may seem. The grievance is important to the complainant. It is also important to you and the organisation: grievances can be a valuable source of feedback.

## Objective

To enable an individual to air a complaint; get to the core of the dissatisfaction and take remedial action, if appropriate.

# Preparation

Often a grievant arrives without any warning! In this case, preparation is not possible. It is important that an interviewer is able to respond effectively rather than reacting emotionally.

Sometimes it is possible to 'keep an ear to the ground'. This is often a good method of identifying potential difficulties before they actually arrive on the doorstep. If you can recognise symptoms quickly, you may be able to avert more serious problems.

If there is a possibility that someone may have a grievance — prepare for it as well as you can. Try to steer the individual into a suitable, accessible room if you are accosted in a public place (corridor; open plan office; shopfloor): it is both difficult and inappropriate to talk with the distractions of background noises and when other people are in close proximity. It is also possible that the individual concerned is angry or upset and may become more emotional. It is easier to deal with this in a more private place.

If you do get some warning of an approaching grievance, find out as much background information as is possible. It may be possible to make some enquiries (be discreet!). Check facts, opinions and attitudes, where appropriate. Check records for any previous situations which were similar.

Make sure you are clear about organisational policy and the limits of your own authority in dealing with the grievance. Especially, make sure you are clear about the organisation's formal grievance procedure in case the interviewee wants to take the matter further. You may want to suggest that the interviewee brings a colleague or appropriate representative with him/her (Union representative, witness, etc.) to the meeting, particularly if it is part of the organisational procedure.

Allow adequate time and ensure privacy where possible. Find out if the interviewee is bringing someone with him/her.

## Skills

The most important point initially is to allow the interviewee to air his/her grievance as soon as possible. Quite often the grievance is not as obvious as the interviewee first thinks it is. It is essential that he/she is assisted to identify the real complaint.

### ACTIVE LISTENING
It is important to use listening skills to initially get the interviewee to explain what has caused the grievance and thereafter to encourage him/her to talk through the problem. Allow the individual to talk freely without interruptions. Remember he/she may be feeling very emotional. It is important that you stay objective about this emotion.

*Listen* to and analyse what is being said. *Listen* for what is *not* said.

*Watch* the interviewee's body language (facial expressions; gestures; posture and eye-contact). Use non-verbal gestures to encourage (eye contact, open body posture, acknowledging noises).

## QUESTIONING

Questioning skills are very important to enable the interviewer to get to the root of the complaint. If you are listening to a grievance use:

- *open* questions initially to get the person to outline the complaint in detail
- *specific* questions to clarify each point made
- *probing* questions to dig deeper and make sure the root cause has been established
- *checking* questions to confirm your understanding of the situation
- *hypothetical* questions to try to help the interviewee to understand other people's point of view. 'If you were in Sally's position, John, how would you have felt?' 'If you feel the system doesn't work, John, how would you improve it?'

## TALKING

Once the initial description of the grievance has been outlined, the interviewee must re-state the complaint as he/she understands it. When you are in a grievance interview, it is essential to make absolutely sure that you have a clear picture of the situation.

Summarising throughout is necessary to make sure that both parties are clear about what has been stated and to enable the discussion to move forward rather than going round in circles.

The interviewer may need to clarify his/her own role and state the organisational policy, if appropriate.

A final summary should be used to ensure complete understanding by both parties of where the discussion has got to and what action is going to be taken next, if appropriate.

## MAKING NOTES

It is important to make a note of the key points about the discussion (the root complaint, summaries and further action). It may also be necessary to draw up a plan of action to remedy the situation. The interviewee should be given copies of the completed notes. Notes are essential if the grievance has to be taken any further (formal grievance procedures).

## EMOTION

It is very likely that a grievant is feeling some emotion: this is quite often anger or frustration. It can be very daunting to be faced with anger or hysteria, but it is essential that the interviewer is able to set an atmosphere of calm reason.

Usually an interviewee is concerned only with telling you about the grievance — to let off steam. If someone is very upset or angry, talking about the problem can help to settle things down. On the other hand, constant interruptions from the interviewer could cause further irritation.

If you are in an interview, don't be tempted to argue heatedly or become emotional yourself. It is important to remain objective and behave assertively. It is surprising how a highly charged situation can calm down when one of the parties is keeping composed and neutral.

# Outcome

If you are able to settle the grievance immediately, it is still important to arrange a follow up meeting to make sure that things have worked out as planned.

Sometimes nothing needs to be done at all. Merely talking about it and letting off steam has enabled someone to accept a situation. Even if this is the case, make a point of having a word with the individual at a later stage, however informally, to check that matters have been resolved.

If the problem has not been resolved, you should state what action is to be taken next as well as a date by which to report results.

If there is no action that you can take and the individual still feels aggrieved, point out the next step of the formal grievance procedure and arrange for a further meeting to take place.

## Follow up

- Investigate facts and discover any other information needed
- Take any action necessary to solve the grievance
- Write up notes from the interview for the record
- Copy notes to the grievant, if appropriate
- Put grievance procedure into motion if necessary
- Check with the individual at a later date to ensure that progress is being made.

## Grievance interview checklist

### OBJECTIVE
To enable a person to air a complaint; get to the core and take action, if appropriate.

## PREPARATION
- Find out as much about the grievance as possible (facts, attitudes, feelings)
- Consult other people for advice
- Check individual's file
- Check for any similar, previous situations
- Confirm own limits of authority; check organisational policy
- Be clear about the organisation's grievance procedure
- Allow for privacy and ensure the location is accessible
- Allocate enough time
- Find out if the individual is bringing a representative.

## SKILLS
- Be calm but positive
- Allow the grievant to let off steam first
- Check your mutual understanding of the exact situation and the facts
- Listen carefully, probe deeply
- Do not belittle the issue or dismiss it
- Finish with positive action for the future, if appropriate. Make sure you are both clear about what happens next
- Make notes.

## FOLLOW UP
- Investigate facts and possible causes of action
- Write notes and copy these to the interviewee
- Arrange a further interview, if appropriate
- Take agreed action.

# 5 the disciplinary interview

A disciplinary interview needs to be conducted fairly and systematically whether it is dealing with what appears to be a minor matter or indeed a more serious situation. If a disciplinary interview is likely to lead to the individual being dismissed, this could be challenged in an industrial tribunal. It is crucial therefore that the interview is treated seriously, fairly and follows the organisational disciplinary procedure. It is also essential that an individual who is the subject of a disciplinary interview is made aware of the disciplinary rules that apply.

For the purpose of this section, we want to take one step back. Before a situation reaches the formal disciplinary procedure stage, there is a time when a less formal discussion can be used to enable an individual to look at ways and means to improve. Discipline is about getting people back on track — it is not about punishment. Nor is it about 'reading the riot act' but more of encouraging improvement to reach acceptable standards when performance levels have slipped below acceptability. The interview is a serious discussion between two people in order to change the behaviour or performance of one of them. Whilst the interviewer needs to treat the occasion seriously, he/she needs also to be firm, pleasant, forgiving but very specific.

## Objective

To discuss with an individual mistakes or inappropriate behaviour which has lead to poor performance with the aim of improving his/her behaviour or work standards and to prevent the situation from arising again.

## Preparation

Whether the problem is a relatively minor one or a more serious one, it is important that careful preparations are made.

The first steps must be:

- to clarify what the offence/shortcomings in performance is/are
- to ensure that the individual is made fully aware of the need for the interview, its status (ie a disciplinary interview) and the reason for the meeting
- to give the individual enough time to prepare for the meeting
- to explain to the individual that he/she has the choice of bringing someone appropriate to the meeting (colleague or Union representative) or coming alone.

# THE DISCIPLINARY INTERVIEW

All the facts must be checked carefully. Read through the job description and/or performance standards for the individual. It is essential, at this stage to be objective: it is important not to prejudge the outcome of the interview until both sides of the story have been heard.

Consider carefully the sanctions available to you and be crystal clear about the stages of the organisational disciplinary procedure. Check the procedure in the handbook, if appropriate. Ensure you are quite clear about the limits of your authority.

Make sure an appropriate room is available (accessible and without interruptions).

Ensure you allow adequate time plus a little contingency.

Gather together any relevant documentation.

## Skills

Explain to the interviewee how the interview will be conducted. It is important at the outset to establish the objective of the interview. Briefly outline the situation as you see it.

### ACTIVE LISTENING

It is important to use listening skills to make sure you get the interviewee's side of the story.

*Listen* to and analyse what is being said. *Listen* for what is *not* said. *Watch* the interviewee's body language (facial expressions; gestures; posture and eye-contact).

## QUESTIONING

Questioning skills are very important to enable the interviewer to get both sides of the story. Use:

- *open* questions to get the person to outline their version of the problem 'What happened when you and John met last week?' It is essential that you are impartial so beware of leading questions such as 'You refused to help John last week, didn't you?'. Use *open* questions again to encourage the interviewee to suggest ways in which improvements will be made
- *closed* questions to establish facts
- *specific* questions to clarify points made
- *probing* questions to dig deeper, if necessary
- *checking* questions to confirm your understanding of the interviewee's statements as well as identify points of action.

## TALKING

Explain the standards of performance expected as well as organisational policy to ensure the interviewee is fully aware of these. If necessary, point out where the interviewee's actions has led to difficulties with colleagues or has had other implications (loss in quality; reduction in customer service; loss of profits).

Summarising throughout is necessary to make sure that both parties are clear about what has been stated. A final summary should be used to ensure complete understanding by both parties of where the discussion has got to and what action is going to be taken next, if appropriate.

Make full notes.

## Making a decision

Once you have re-looked at all the facts and reviewed the discussions at the interview you should make a decision.

- Is the employee to be given a warning and the full disciplinary procedure to be implemented?
- Whether the answer is 'yes' or 'no' — what action is to be taken to help the individual to improve/avoid further mistakes?
- When is the person to be seen again — allowing a reasonable time in which to improve so that the same offence will not be committed again?

Make sure that future action has been clearly understood by the interviewee. Confirm decision and action in writing.

Disciplinary interviews should be approached according to the stage of procedure reached. An informal, problem-solving approach is often best at the initial stage or where the offence is minor. Considerate handling at the initial stages often prevents the procedure from having to go further. The atmosphere will need to become more formal if disciplinary action continues towards the final stage.

## Follow up

Write up your notes immediately after the interview. Record any warning given and send copies to the individual. Make an appointment with the interviewee to review behaviour/performance.

# Disciplinary interview checklist

## OBJECTIVE

To discuss with an individual mistakes or inappropriate behaviour which need correcting and identifying ways in which specific improvements can be made.

## PREPARATION
- Be clear about the reasons for seeing the person
- Get all the facts
- Don't prejudge
- Consider sanctions available
- Know the procedure
- Ensure privacy
- Allow enough time
- Gather together all the relevant documentation
- Let interviewee know he/she is entitled to have a representative present.

## SKILLS
- State the reason for and the objective of the meeting
- Ask interviewee for his/her side of the story
- Probe and clarify
- Keep calm, firm and fair.

## FOLLOW UP
- Write up notes immediately and file
- Give copy of decision to interviewee

# THE DISCIPLINARY INTERVIEW

- Send out copies of warnings given
- Make appointment for follow up interview
- Take any action agreed on to help the individual.

# 6 the appraisal interview

The appraisal interview has been around for some time: unfortunately time doesn't necessarily mean it has been perfected. An appraisal interview, if conducted properly, can be beneficial to everyone as well as the organisation as a whole. Relations between those involved can be strengthened as a result of the two-way communication involved in the process.

On the other hand, a badly conducted appraisal can lead easily to mistrust and suspicion on the part of the interviewee, which, in turn, leads to a lack of co-operation and interest at the interview.

When appraisals were first introduced, they put fear and dread into the minds of some people: an interview was like a 'dark cloud' hanging over them at a particular time every year or so. 'The dreaded appraisal with my boss: what have I done wrong?' More recently, appraisals have become less rigid. They may be conducted semi-formally throughout the year with a more formal review at the year end. New types of appraisal have been introduced including the revolutionary 360° appraisal where individuals receive feedback on their behaviour and performance from their staff and peers as well as their managers.

An appraisal gives the opportunity to:

- take stock and do some self assessment (on the part of the appraisee)
- reflect on past performance
- look at all round achievements, give due recognition and look to the future.

For the purpose of this booklet, we will assume that an appraisal is an interview carried out between an individual and his/her boss.

## Objective

The appraisal interview often fails because the interviewer is mistaken about the objective. It is not '..to fill in the form' or 'to tell the person where he/she went wrong'. Generally, it is a two-way exchange of information between two parties which is related to one individual's performance over a given period of time. There are a number of different objectives for carrying out an appraisal. These include:

- assessing performance against agreed standards/objectives
- identifying strengths and weaknesses
- building on strengths and overcoming weaknesses
- identifying areas for improvement
- identifying training and development needs

- planning and setting standards/objectives for the future
- discussing future aspirations and motivations.

Ideally, an appraisal shouldn't be linked directly to pay reviews or salary increases: it is about past performance, current progress and future plans. If the results of an appraisal do influence pay, the appraisee is unlikely to be open and honest about areas of difficulty or to voice criticisms of the organisation or manager. However, where performance-related pay schemes are in operation, evidence of individuals' achievement of objectives may be used to determine awards.

## Preparation

Preparation is essential: for both the manager and the job holder.

A date should be arranged with the appraisees which gives a minimum of one week's leeway, so that they can prepare for the meeting. Often the appraisees are given either the appraisal form to complete the appropriate sections or an appraisal preparation form to help clarify thoughts before the meeting.

Otherwise they should be asked to prepare for the interview by considering some points:

- their performance over the previous 12 months: if they have been working to a set of objectives, then performance should be assessed against achievement of these

# THE APPRAISAL INTERVIEW

- their areas of particular achievement and any problem areas
- future ambitions and areas of self-development leading to specific training/development
- any thoughts on changes to the job itself
- any ways in which management can assist.

The appraiser needs to:

- review the job description and standards of performance/objectives
- check the objectives and/or targets set at the last appraisal (or in the interim) and note the results
- identify areas of strengths
- assess any weaknesses and get any background information on these (was it a management problem or caused by someone else?)
- check that any training/development needs agreed at the previous appraisal have been met (if not, why not?)
- clarify if identified short term aspirations have been met (if not, why not?).

A suitable room needs to be arranged.

It is essential that the room is completely private and there will not be interruptions. Try to make the seating arrangements fairly informal. However, there needs to be a balance: an appraisal is not a cosy chat (if a table is used, then both parties should sit at the same side or at adjoining sides: not facing each other).

## Skills

It is essential that the objective of the interview is stressed together with the two-way nature of the occasion.

### QUESTIONING
The appraisee should be encouraged to talk and express his/her thoughts. Use:

- *open* questions to establish feelings about the job
- *specific* and *closed* questions to find out how the job has been over the period in question as well as to establish facts
- *reflective* questions to encourage the interviewee to expand on points.

Beware *leading* questions: these can lead to the appraisee telling you what you want to hear, and not what he/she actually thinks.

### ACTIVE LISTENING
One of the biggest mistakes of an appraisal is for the interviewer to do most of the talking. It is an opportunity for the appraisee to reflect on his/her job and the period of the appraisal: this means he/she is the main talker. It is important for the appraiser to listen carefully; observe body language and give encouragement through his/her own body language. The objective is not 'to tell him/her where he/she has gone wrong': it is not an adversarial occasion nor is it a disciplinary interview.

## TALKING

This is a combination of making statements about the person's performance, identifying objectives and directions for the future and summarising.

Reflecting on what went before shouldn't happen until the appraisee has given his/her view. There is a great danger that the 'tell' approach will cut off any contribution from the employee. Putting your view first can make interviewees feel that there is no point in giving their opinion because you have already made up your mind.

The purpose should be to add to the employee's points, rather than submerge them. It is a time for looking at all round achievements and giving due recognition to all aspects: not just those that find favour.

## ACTION PLANNING

Review dates: new objectives/targets — success criteria — enables follow up. Targets should be set for the next period — both short and long term.

Points should be summarised as they are dealt with and a final summary should be used to emphasise conclusions and future action.

## BUILDING A RAPPORT

It is most important that the appraisee feels relaxed and goes away feeling that the interview was a positive and worthwhile experience.

If 'poor performance' has to be discussed, it should not come as a surprise to the appraisee. It should be something that he/she has been made aware of previously: this is a time for looking at it in terms of whether any improvements have been made already and what further means can be used to continue that process. It should not be an occasion for acknowledging problems. Try to maintain a level of informality so that it is a purposeful two-way discussion rather than an inquisition.

## Follow up

The first stage of the process is to complete the appraisal form. Ideally, this should be a draft which is passed to the interviewee for approval. Once it has been agreed it should be finalised and signed by the appraisee. A copy should be given to him/her.

There are occasions when agreement may not be reached. There should be a process available by which the appraisee is able to 'appeal'. This depends on the organisation but very often it is a 'grandparent' system (the manager of the manager involved in the interview). If final agreement cannot be agreed, then the appraisee may make a note on the appraisal and sign to this effect.

Any action agreed during the interview (for the appraiser) should be taken (training courses; job rotation/shadowing/expansion). Action by the appraisee is part of his/her self-development and is the appraisee's responsibility. However, that doesn't suggest abdication: the appraiser should keep an eye on how the interviewee is doing. Any action identified for you, along with target dates should be followed up.

## Appraisal interview checklist

OBJECTIVE
To review an employee's performance over a given period in order to:

- Assess performance against agreed standards/objectives
- Identify strengths and weaknesses
- Build on strengths and overcoming weaknesses
- Identify areas for improvement
- Identify training and development needs
- Plan and setting standards/objectives for the future
- Discuss future aspirations and motivations.

PREPARATION
- Give appraisee time to prepare
- Check job description, previous appraisal and targets set
- Note strengths and weaknesses
- Think of ways improvements could be achieved
- Arrange for a private, accessible room
- Decide on duration and ensure no interruptions.

SKILLS
- Ask open questions to encourage the appraisee to talk
- Use reflective questions to encourage expansion
- Use closed and specific questions to establish facts and encourage self-assessment by the appraisee
- Listen actively

- Make statements once the interviewee has reflected on his/her performance
- Summarise throughout and at the end.

FOLLOW UP
- Set short and long term target dates
- Complete forms
- Take agreed own action and monitor appraisee's action.

# 7 the exit interview

There was a time when a 'job was for life': nowadays people move around much more frequently, particularly when development or promotional opportunities are only available outside their current positions. Of course, there are also less positive reasons for moving on.

Whether the reason for moving on is positive or negative, exit interviews are an important source of valuable feedback for organisations. They can provide information on:

- the quality of the recruitment and selection process (whether it is working effectively or improvements need to be made)
- organisational issues (unsolved grievances/ problems; policies and procedures; working conditions; salary scales)
- the quality of management (acceptable/could be improved)
- the level of training and development (opportunities/lack of opportunities).

## Objective

- To discover a person's real reason for resigning
- To improve the selection procedure and reduce staff turnover (if appropriate)
- To gain information on whether the design of the job should be changed
- To secure the employee's goodwill by wishing him/her well
- To persuade an individual to change his/her mind (on occasions).

## Preparation

- Check the letter of resignation
- Review the personal file
- Is the letter reasonable according to your knowledge of the person?
- Reflect on his/her past history
- If there is an exit interview form, make sure you have one to hand.

## Skills

Explain the purpose of the interview at the outset. Keep it informal.

### QUESTIONING

Ask open questions to try to expand on the reasons given in the resignation letter. Often the reason stated is not the full story or even the real reason.

Use probing questions to go deeper and get further detail of the reasons for leaving.

If appropriate, work through the form questions but without making it seem like an inquisition. Remember, it should be fairly informal.

### ACTIVE LISTENING

Listen and observe carefully. Often a resignation is a final cry for help or attention.

Make sure the individual's body language is in line with what he/she is saying.

### TALKING

You may be trying to change the interviewee's mind: you may want to point out the advantages and opportunities of his/her remaining.

Finally, wish the individual well: even if you have failed to persuade him/her to stay.

It does no one any good to send an ex-employee away with a 'bitter taste in his/her mouth'.

## Follow up

Decide if action is necessary in the light of any information gained. Implement action. Any criticisms should be noted and action taken later. However, if there are more serious comments (suggestions of: bullying or discrimination) then an immediate investigation will have to be taken as well as a more formal statement from the leaver.

# The exit interview checklist

### OBJECTIVE
- To discover a person's real reason for resigning
- To improve the selection procedure and reduce staff turnover (if appropriate)
- To secure the employee's goodwill by wishing him/her well
- To persuade an individual to change his/her mind (on occasions).

### PREPARATION
- Check letter of resignation
- Study personal file
- Check room for privacy and accessibility
- Allow plenty of time.

### SKILLS
- Ask open and probing questions
- Be friendly
- Listen carefully and observe body language
- Thank and wish well.

### FOLLOW UP
- Decide if any action needs to be taken as a result.

# appendices

## Appendix 1: Job description framework

**Job Title:**

**Accountable to:**

**Accountable for:**

**Job Purpose:**

**Achievement areas/Key result areas**

- 
- 
- 
- 
- 
- 
- 

**Budgetary limits:**

**Limits of authority:**

# Appendix 2: Person specification framework

| | **Essential** *(The abilities, attributes, etc. that are absolutely crucial to the job)* | **Desirable** *(The abilities, attributes, further experience, etc. that would make it easier for the job holder to become effective more quickly. However, the job could be done without them)* |
|---|---|---|

**Education/qualifications**
(Academic/Vocational/Professional educational achievements; CPD - continuous professional development)

**Work/relevant experience**
(Attainments, specialist knowledge, skills and application)

# APPENDICES

**Interests/aspirations**
(Main interests, motivations, ambitions)

**Personal qualities/abilities**
(Initiative, interpersonal relationships, leadership)

**Circumstances**
(Background, willingness and ability to move/travel, work irregular hours)

## Person specification example: Admin clerk — accounting

| | **Essential** (The abilities, attributes, etc. that are absolutely crucial to the job) | **Desirable** (The abilities, attributes, further experience, etc that would make it easier for the job holder to become effective more quickly. However, the job could be done without them) |
|---|---|---|
| **Education/qualifications** (Academic/Vocational/Professional educational achievements) | GCSE English language or equivalent; numeracy (basic calculations and statistics) | GCSE Maths or equivalent |
| **Work/relevant experience** (Attainments, specialist knowledge, skills and application) | Clerical experience preferably in an accountancy firm; computer literacy | Experience of Excel; Access and Microsoft Word. NVQ in Administration Level 2 |
| **Interests/aspirations** (Main interests, motivations, ambitions) | Self-motivation; sociability | Willingness to learn |

# APPENDICES

| | | |
|---|---|---|
| **Personal qualities/abilities** (Initiative, inter-personal relationships, leadership) | Can communicate face to face to face/on the telephone; ability to work with others/as part of a team; organisational ability; good time management; trustworthiness | Ability to set own objectives |
| **Circumstances** (Background, willingness and ability to move/travel, work irregular hours) | Ability to work flexitime; non-smoker | Own transport as public facilities poor |

# Appendix 3:
# Interview assessment form framework

**Candidate name:** Vacancy:

**Interview/s** Interview date:

Essential  Desirable  Rating (1 = Poor; 2 = Fair; 3 = Good; 4 = Excellent)

**Education/qualifications** (Academic/ Vocational/ Professional educational achievements)

**Work/relevant experience** (Attainments, specialist knowledge, skills and application)

## APPENDICES

**Interests/aspirations**
(Main interests, motivations, ambitions)

**Personal qualities/abilities**
(Initiative, interpersonal relationships, leadership)

**Circumstances**
(Background, willingness and ability to move/travel, work irregular hours)

# Appendix 4: Key items for inclusion in an application form

Different organisations have a variety of ways of presenting application forms: some have more than one. Which one is used depends on the type and level of job. However, there are some headings which should included in any application form:

- Job applied for
- Name, address and telephone number
- Academic/vocational/professional achievements
- Training and Qualifications
- Employment history and experience
- Equal opportunities monitoring section (This could be separate or detachable.)
- Additional information (anything candidate would wish to include in support of his/her application)
- Place for a signature and the date with the words 'I confirm that the information contained in this application is correct'.

# Appendix 5: Legislation affecting the interview process

## THE DISABILITY DISCRIMINATION ACT 1995

These provisions replace the Register of disabled people and Quota Designated Employment Schemes set up under the 1994 Act. The Act covers two main areas affecting employment:

- making it unlawful for employers with 20 or more employees to discriminate on the grounds of disability against current or prospective employees
- requiring employers to make reasonable adjustments to their employment arrangements or premises if they substantially disadvantage disabled employees or applicants.

Employers must not discriminate against disabled people in the areas of:

- recruitment (job advertisement, interviewing, shortlisting and selection procedures)
- promotion, retention and transfer
- training and career development opportunities
- dismissal
- redundancy (unless all employees are made redundant on the same grounds)
- premises and employment arrangements.

Discrimination is defined as treating a disabled person less favourably than someone else, where:

- the reason given relates to the person's disability and does not therefore apply to the other person
- the treatment cannot be justified.

However, less favourable treatment of a disabled person can be justified if:

- the treatment is relevant to the circumstances of the individual case
- the reason for the treatment is substantial (rather than minor or trivial) and cannot be reduced or overcome by making a reasonable adjustment.

## REHABILITATION OF OFFENDERS ACT 1974

Currently, an ex-offender, after a period of rehabilitation, has no need to disclose a previous conviction unless his sentence exceeds 2½ years imprisonment. Once a conviction becomes 'spent', an employer cannot refuse to employ, dismiss or otherwise discriminate against an ex-offender on the grounds of a previous conviction.

The above might be affected in the near future. The Government White Paper 'On the Record: The Government's Proposals for Access to Criminal Records for Employment and Related Purposes in England and Wales' details proposals for access to criminal records for employment and related purposes. A proposed Code of Practice is annexed to the White Paper setting out guidance for employers regarding applications for full and enhanced checks on criminal records. Employers will be expected to abide by this Code of Practice.

The White Paper proposes the setting up of a Criminal Record Agency (CRA) which will undertake criminal record checks. If the bill becomes law, candidates will have to provide a Criminal Conviction Certificate (CCC) which shows unspent convictions. A CCC will not include cautions or convictions which are 'spent' under the Rehabilition of Offenders Act. Employers will be able to ask individuals to produce a certificate, although it is not intended that this should be mandatory.

The White Paper is available from HMSO.

## SEX DISCRIMINATION ACT 1975 (AND 1986)

The Act made it illegal for employers, professional bodies and trade unions to discriminate either directly or indirectly on the grounds of sex or marital status except where a particular sex or marital status could be shown to be a bona fide requirement as defined under the legislation. Similarly, it became illegal to place an advertisement indicating an intention to discriminate either directly or by implication (indirectly).

## RACE RELATIONS ACT 1976

The objectives of the Act were to eliminate patterns of racial discrimination and remedy individual grievances. To this end the complaints machinery was strengthened and the new Commission for Racial Equality was given considerable powers of investigation in addition to increased enforcement powers. Direct or indirect discrimination is unlawful on the grounds of race, ethnic or national origins, in the fields of employment, education facilities and services and housing, and in clubs with more than 25 members, and which is to the detriment of the person discriminated against.

## FAIR EMPLOYMENT (NI) ACT 1989
Employers in Northern Ireland must not discriminate against candidates on religious grounds, specifically because they are Protestants or Catholics.

## ASYLUM AND IMMIGRATION ACT 1996 — SECTION 8
This requires organisations to keep documentary evidence of an applicant's legal right to work in the United Kingdom. It takes effect in relation to employees who start work on or after 27th January 1997. It means that an employer could be guilty of a criminal offence if they employ someone who does not have permission to be in — or work in — the United Kingdom.